This book belong

_____

Paperback ISBN: 978-1-63731-670-2
Hardcover ISBN: 978-1-63731-672-6
eBook ISBN: 978-1-63731-671-9

Printed and bound in the USA.
NinjaLifeHacks.tv

Ninja Life Hacks®
by Mary Nhin

Entrepreneur Ninja

A Book About Developing an Entrepreneurial Mindset

Passion

Idea

Help

Solutions

Problem

Business

Ninja Life Hacks
by Mary Nhin

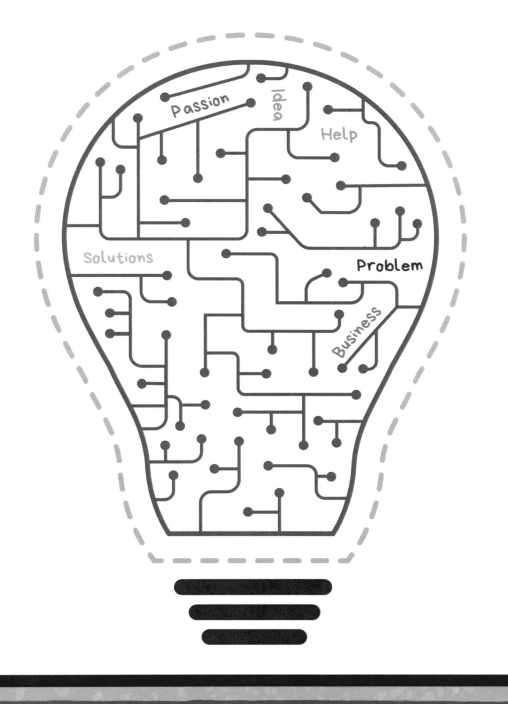

Mars Elevator: a door that transports you to your alternate home in Mars.

Before I created these businesses, I didn't have the slightest idea on how to be an entrepreneur! Then one day, Inventor Ninja and Innovative Ninja shared with me some tips on inventions and innovation. After some trial, practice, and deep thinking, I created a strategy called the 4 Fs!

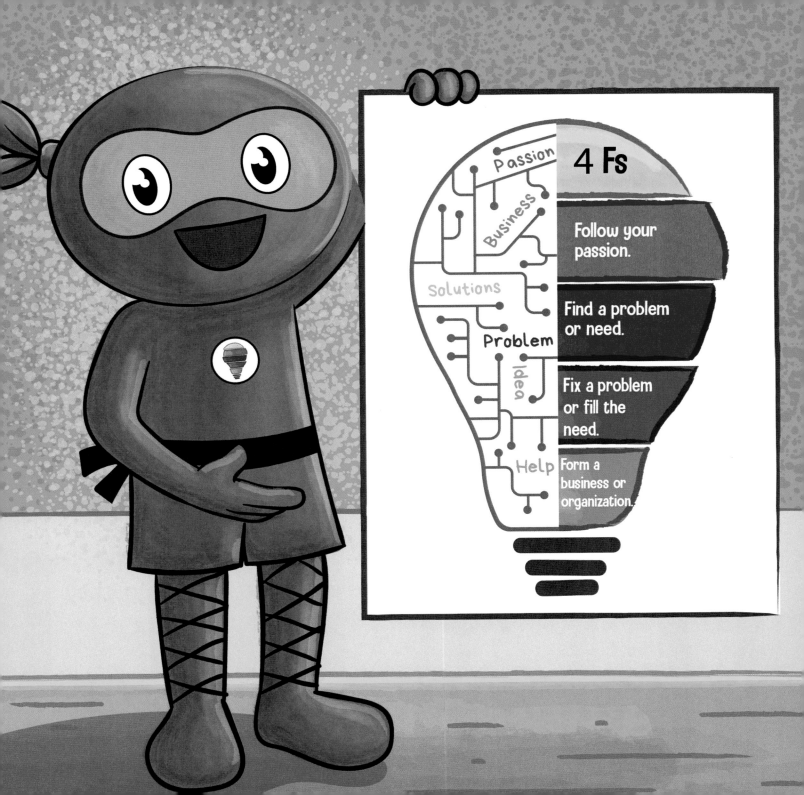

Form

For the last step, you'll **form** a business or organization to help share your solution with the world. You may choose to ask an adult for help. You'll want to create a business name and logo which will usually hint to what the business is about or stands for.

The McDonald's symmetrical logo has a line of symmetry along the y-axis.

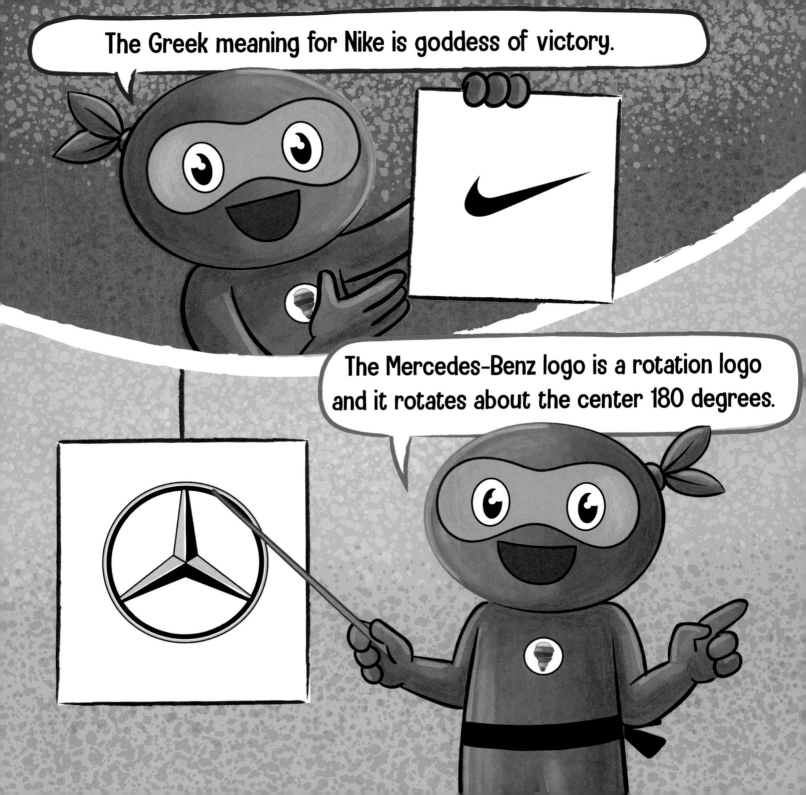

Mary Nhin loves being the guinea pig for all her husband's kitchen creations. She is a mom of three boys, serial entrepreneur, and author. She has a passion for helping children develop confidence and grow grit. Her books have sold over 4 million copies worldwide.

Email her your thoughts and suggestions at info@ninjalifehacks.tv and follow @officialninjalifehacks on IG/FB/TT.

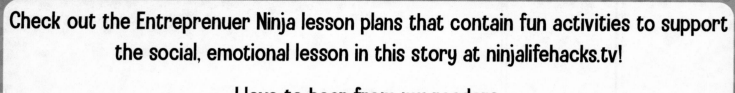

Check out the Entreprenuer Ninja lesson plans that contain fun activities to support the social, emotional lesson in this story at ninjalifehacks.tv!

I love to hear from my readers.
Write to me at info@ninjalifehacks.tv or send me mail at:

Mary Nhin
6608 N Western Avenue #1166
Oklahoma City, OK 73116

Made in United States
Orlando, FL
28 May 2025

61648536R00021